My life story:

....

Everyone, as they say, has at least one book inside them! This book aims to tease out the brilliant memoir inside you!

...but writing your autobiography or memoir is no easy matter! Right?

Where do you start?
What do you include?
How should you organize it?

This book aims to take some of the stress out of that whole 'staring at a blank page' feeling and get you started writing!

For each life stage there are some prompts or questions – some rather deep and some more light-hearted! Use as many or as few as you feel like – this is your book!

You may find that there are things which you haven't thought about in decades and others that happened just last week that you want to include. The book is sectioned up already so that you can jump from one era to another as you please.

Whether you're writing down your life experiences for yourself, your children, your grandchildren or your great-grandchildren the result could be illuminating/entertaining/surprising. Who knows...?

So ... turn over and let's get started...

Teen years: 88

- ☞ Which secondary school did you attend? What's something that happened to you at school that you'll always remember?
- ☞ Most/least favourite subjects/teachers.
- ☞ First boyfriend/girlfriend/kiss...
- ☞ What was your favourite music? How did you listen to music as a teenager?
- ☞ Did you have your own bedroom growing up, or did you share with a sibling? Describe your room.
- ☞ What was the best/most memorable party you went to when you were a teenager?
- ☞ Do you remember any fads from your youth? Popular hairstyles? Clothes?
- ☞ How were your belief systems formed? (religion, politics, family, etc.)

Adult life: 128

- ☞ What film/song was Number 1 on your 21st birthday?
- ☞ What did you do after you left school?
- ☞ Can you offer a behind-the-scenes look at a particular job? How did the work affect you? Is there a message concerning a type of work you've done?
- ☞ When and how did you meet your spouse/partner? How would you describe your spouse/partner? What did you do on dates?
- ☞ What's an incident that changed how you think or feel about something?
- ☞ What's an incident that changed your life?
- ☞ What's a time or place when it felt as if your heart were breaking?
- ☞ What world events have had the most impact on you as an adult? Did any of them personally affect your family?
- ☞ Describe the most unusual or memorable place you have lived.

Later life: 168

- ☞ When is the last time you learned to do something new?
- ☞ Can you remember a time you learned to do something, or did something for the first time?
- ☞ What lessons have you learned? Do you have a message for the next generation?
- ☞ How many life goals have you attained?
- ☞ Is there something you've done that you want to get off your chest? Will your revelation help others?
- ☞ What's a time or place that you laughed a lot?
- ☞ What memories emerge when you make a time line of your life so far and note the most important things that happened to you each year?
- ☞ How is the world today different from what it was like when you were a child?

Thoughts/quotes/sayings: 198

- ☞ Write about some sayings, expressions, or advice you heard at home when you were growing up. Who said them? What did they mean? Do you use any of those expressions today?
- ☞ Write about some sayings, expressions, or advice you've heard as an adult that have a resonance for you.

Family stories: 218

- ☞ What do you know about your family surname?
- ☞ What stories have come down to you about your parents? Grandparents? More distant ancestors?
- ☞ Are there any stories about famous or infamous relatives in your family?
- ☞ Do you have quirky or interesting relatives on your family tree? Describe one or two of them.

Anything else?

☞ _____ ____

☞ _____ ____

☞ _____ ____

☞ _____ ____

☞ _____ ____

☞ _____ ____

☞ _____ ____

☞ _____ ____

Childhood – Birth/Early years

Childhood – Birth/Early years

Childhood – Birth/Early years

Childhood – Birth/Early years

Childhood – Birth/Early years

Childhood – Birth/Early years

Childhood – Birth/Early years

Childhood – Birth/Early years

Childhood – Birth/Early years

Childhood – Birth/Early years

Childhood – Birth/Early years

Childhood – Birth/Early years

Childhood – Birth/Early years

Childhood – Birth/Early years

Childhood – Birth/Early years

Childhood – Birth/Early years

Childhood – Birth/Early years

Childhood – Birth/Early years

Childhood – Birth/Early years

Childhood – Birth/Early years

Childhood – Birth/Early years

Childhood – Birth/Early years

Childhood – Birth/Early years

Childhood – Birth/Early years

Childhood – Birth/Early years

Childhood – Birth/Early years

Childhood – Birth/Early years

Childhood – Birth/Early years

Childhood – Birth/Early years

Childhood – Birth/Early years

Childhood – Birth/Early years

Childhood – Birth/Early years

Childhood – Birth/Early years

Childhood – Birth/Early years

Childhood – Birth/Early years

Childhood – Birth/Early years

Childhood – Birth/Early years

Childhood – Birth/Early years

Childhood – Birth/Early years

Childhood – Birth/Early years

Childhood – 5 - 12 years

Childhood – 5 - 12 years

Childhood – 5 - 12 years

Childhood – 5 - 12 years

Childhood – 5 - 12 years

Childhood – 5 - 12 years

Childhood – 5 - 12 years

Childhood – 5 - 12 years

Childhood – 5 - 12 years

Childhood – 5 - 12 years

Childhood – 5 - 12 years

Childhood – 5 - 12 years

Childhood – 5 - 12 years

Childhood – 5 - 12 years

Childhood – 5 - 12 years

Childhood – 5 - 12 years

Childhood – 5 - 12 years

Childhood – 5 - 12 years

Childhood – 5 - 12 years

Childhood – 5 - 12 years

Childhood – 5 - 12 years

Childhood – 5 - 12 years

Childhood – 5 - 12 years

Childhood – 5 - 12 years

Childhood – 5 - 12 years

Childhood – 5 - 12 years

Childhood – 5 - 12 years

Childhood – 5 - 12 years

Childhood – 5 - 12 years

Childhood – 5 - 12 years

Childhood – 5 - 12 years

Childhood – 5 - 12 years

Childhood – 5 - 12 years

Childhood – 5 - 12 years

Childhood – 5 - 12 years

Childhood – 5 - 12 years

Childhood – 5 - 12 years

Childhood – 5 - 12 years

Childhood – 5 - 12 years

Childhood – 5 - 12 years

Teen years

Teen years

Teen years

Teen years

Teen years

Teen years

Teen years

Teen years

Teen years

Teen years

Teen years

Teen years

Teen years

Teen years

Teen years

Teen years

Teen years

Teen years

Teen years

Teen years

Teen years

Teen years

Teen years

Teen years

Teen years

Teen years

Teen years

Teen years

Teen years

Teen years

Teen years

Teen years

Teen years

Teen years

Teen years

Teen years

Teen years

Teen years

Teen years

Teen years

Adult life

Adult life

Adult life

Adult life

Adult life

Adult life

Adult life

Adult life

Adult life

Adult life

Adult life

Adult life

Adult life

Adult life

Adult life

Adult life

Adult life

Adult life

Adult life

Adult life

Adult life

Adult life

Adult life

Adult life

Adult life

Adult life

Adult life

Adult life

Adult life

Adult life

Adult life

Adult life

Adult life

Adult life

Adult life

Adult life

Adult life

Adult life

Adult life

Adult life

Later life

Later life

Later life

Later life

Later life

Later life

Later life

Later life

Later life

Later life

Later life

Later life

Later life

Later life

Later life

Later life

Later life

Later life

Later life

Later life

Later life

Later life

Later life

Later life

Later life

Later life

Later life

Later life

Later life

Later life

Thoughts/Quotes/Sayings

Thoughts/Quotes/Sayings

Thoughts/Quotes/Sayings

Thoughts/Quotes/Sayings

Thoughts/Quotes/Sayings

Thoughts/Quotes/Sayings

Thoughts/Quotes/Sayings

Thoughts/Quotes/Sayings

Thoughts/Quotes/Sayings

Thoughts/Quotes/Sayings

Thoughts/Quotes/Sayings

Thoughts/Quotes/Sayings

Thoughts/Quotes/Sayings

Thoughts/Quotes/Sayings

Thoughts/Quotes/Sayings

Thoughts/Quotes/Sayings

Thoughts/Quotes/Sayings

Thoughts/Quotes/Sayings

Thoughts/Quotes/Sayings

Thoughts/Quotes/Sayings

Family stories

Family stories

Family stories

Family stories

Family stories

Family stories

Family stories

Family stories

Family stories

Family stories

Family stories

Family stories

Family stories

Family stories

Family stories

Family stories

Family stories

Family stories

Family stories

Family stories

Family stories

Family stories

Family stories

Family stories

Family stories

Family stories

Family stories

Family stories

Family stories

Family stories

Anything else

Anything else

Anything else

Anything else

Anything else

Anything else

Anything else

Family stories

Family stories

Anything else

Anything else

Anything else

Anything else

Anything else

Anything else

Anything else

Anything else

Anything else

Anything else

Anything else

Anything else

Anything else

Anything else

Anything else

Anything else

Anything else

Anything else

Anything else

Anything else

Anything else

Anything else

Anything else

Anything else

Anything else

Anything else

Anything else

Anything else

Anything else

Anything else

Anything else

Anything else

Anything else

Anything else

Printed in Great Britain
by Amazon

36030445R00165